NATURE COLORING BOOK

INSPIRED BY THE PACIFIC NORTHWEST

BY TRIXY EICHLER

This coloring book is dedicated to Mathias, Sam, and Ruby.

Thanks for all the adventures!

NATURE COLORING BOOK
Inspired by the Pacific Northwest

First Edition

Author: Trixy Eichler

Copyright: All artwork, images, graphics and text © Trixy Eichler, 2016. All rights reserved.

No part of this book may be used, reproduced in any matter whatsover without written permission from the publisher. Please contact me.

Contact: trixwithay.com

Publisher: The Outdoor Society for TRIXWITHAY

The mountains and forests of the Pacific Northwest are overflowing with lush greenery, vivid wild flowers, and icy landscapes.

You might be familiar with this beautiful landscape or you have yet to experience a hike through the rain forest or a brisk climb to a peak.

I invite you to grab a handful of pencils and use your memories or imagination to turn these pages into your own version of this special corner of the world.

Trixy Eichler
TRIXWITHAY

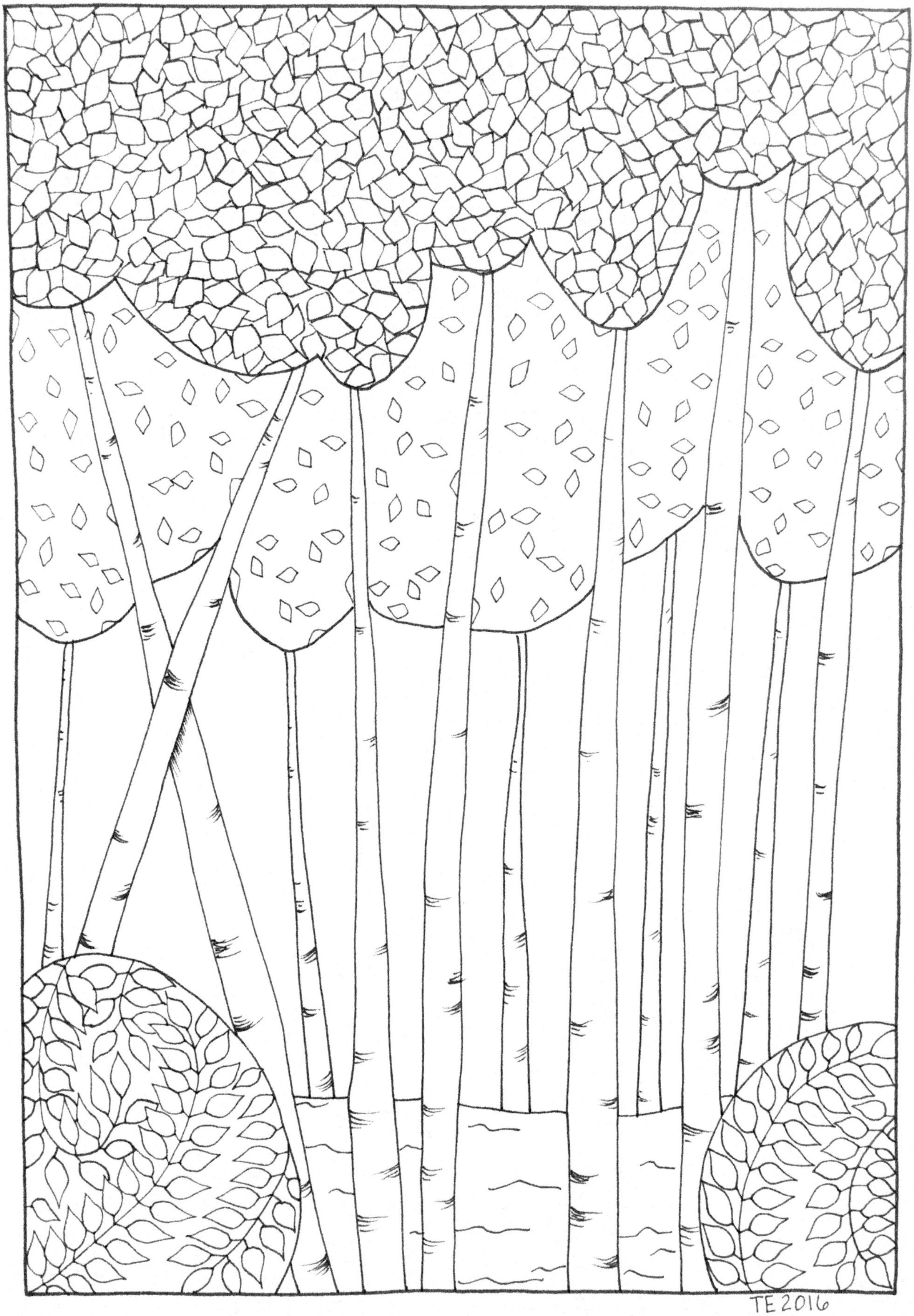

TE 2016

TE 2016

TE 2016

TE 2016

TE 2016

TE 2016

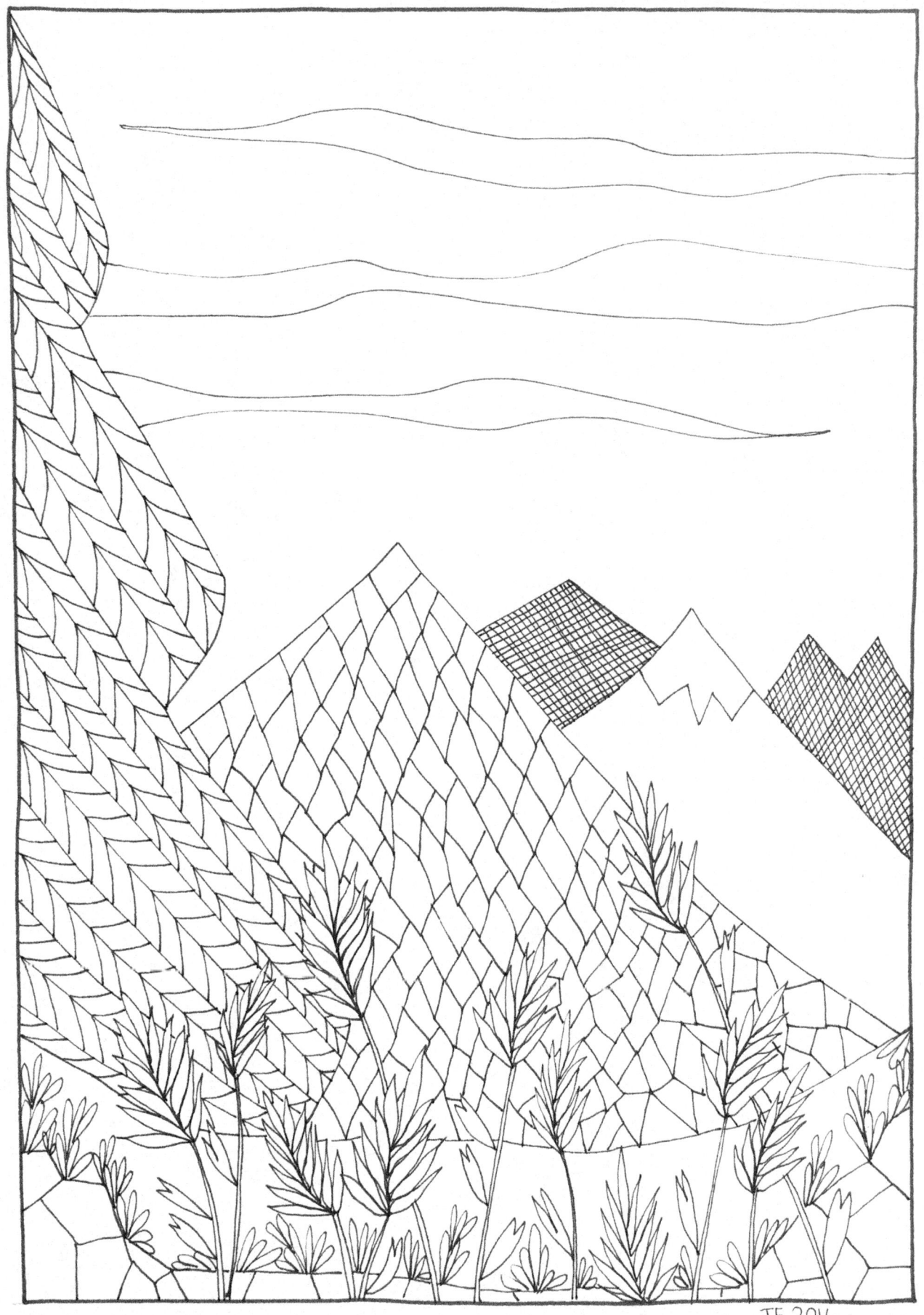

TE 2016

TE 2016

TE 2016

TE 2016

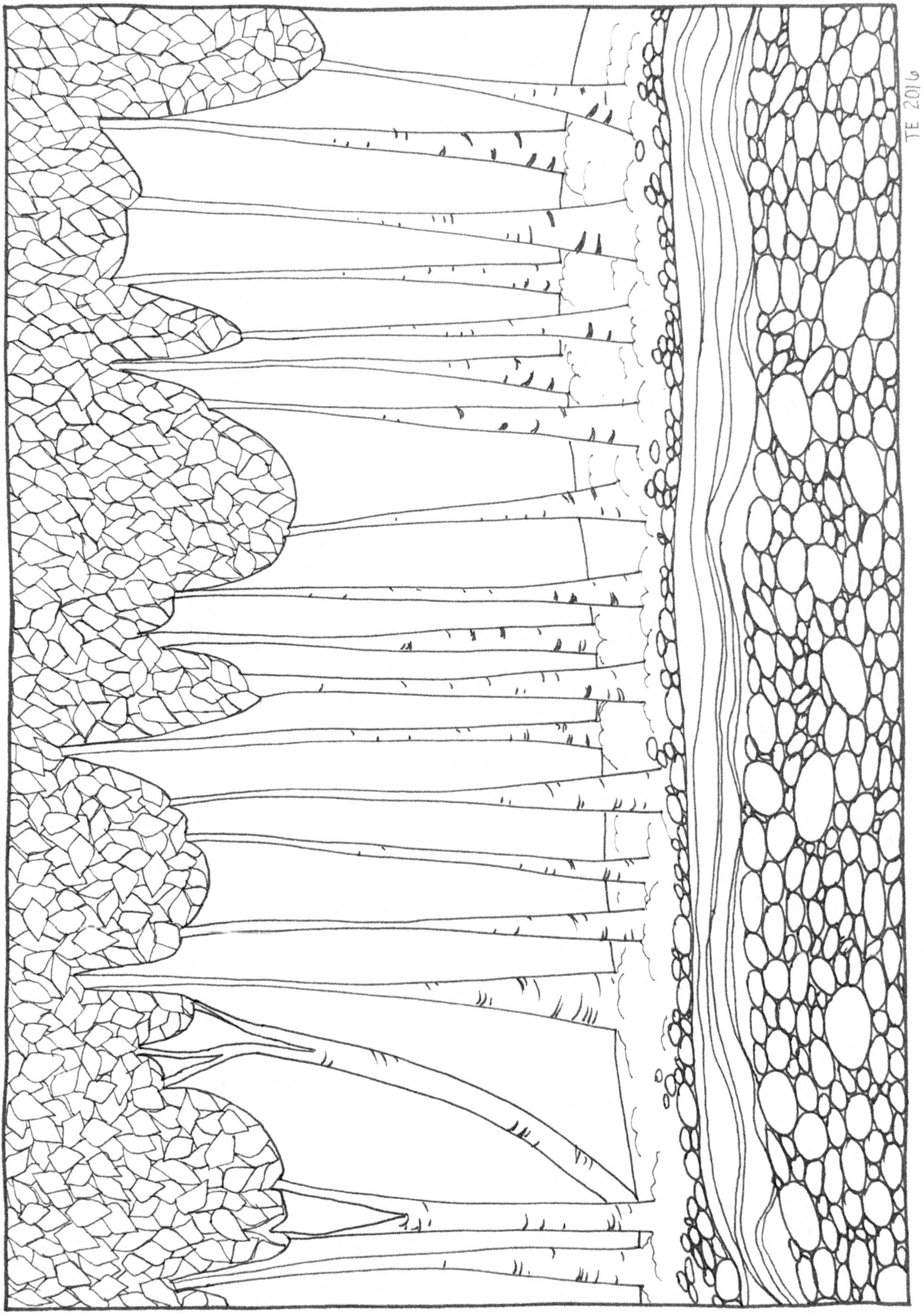
TE 2016

TE 2016

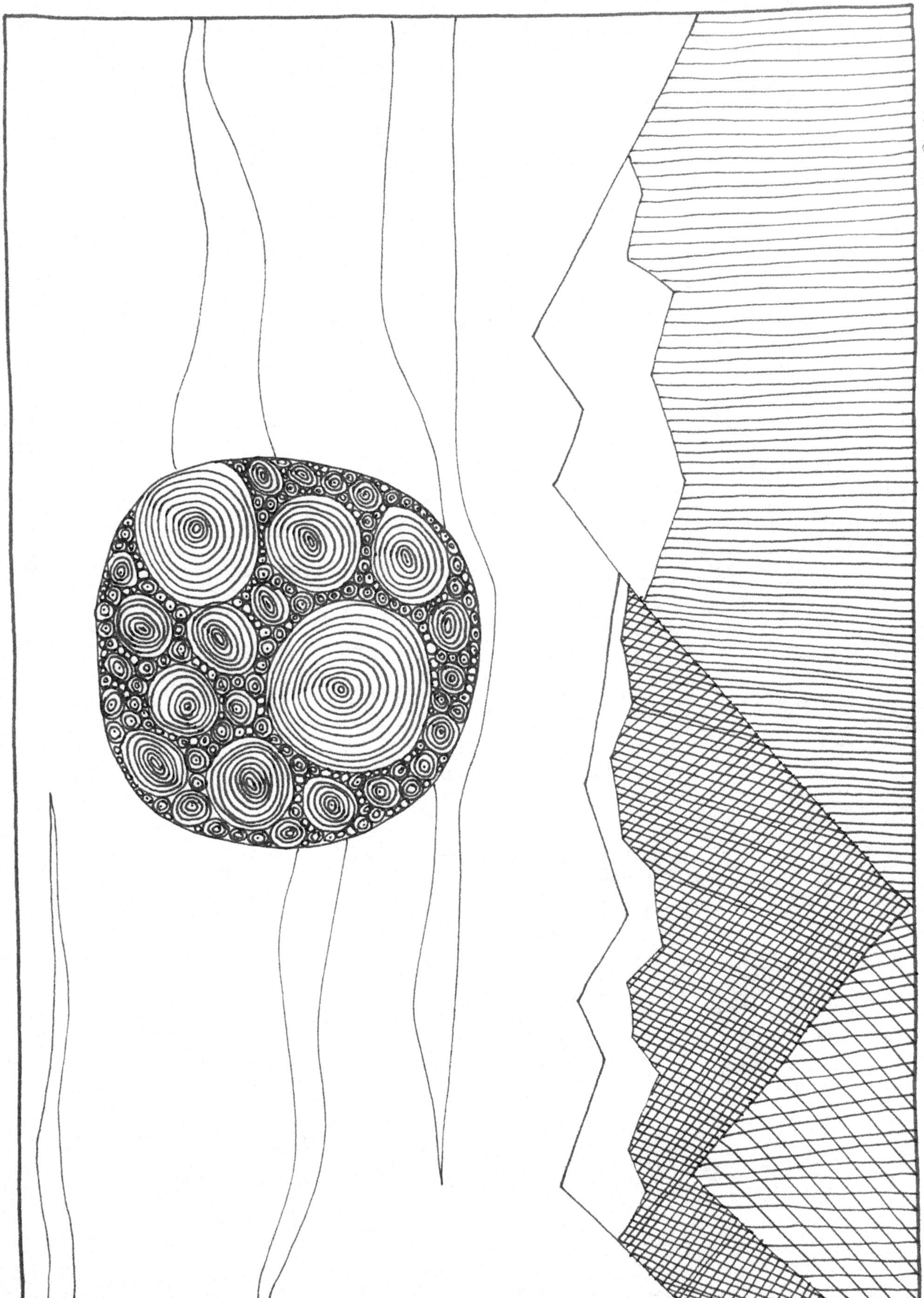
TE 2016

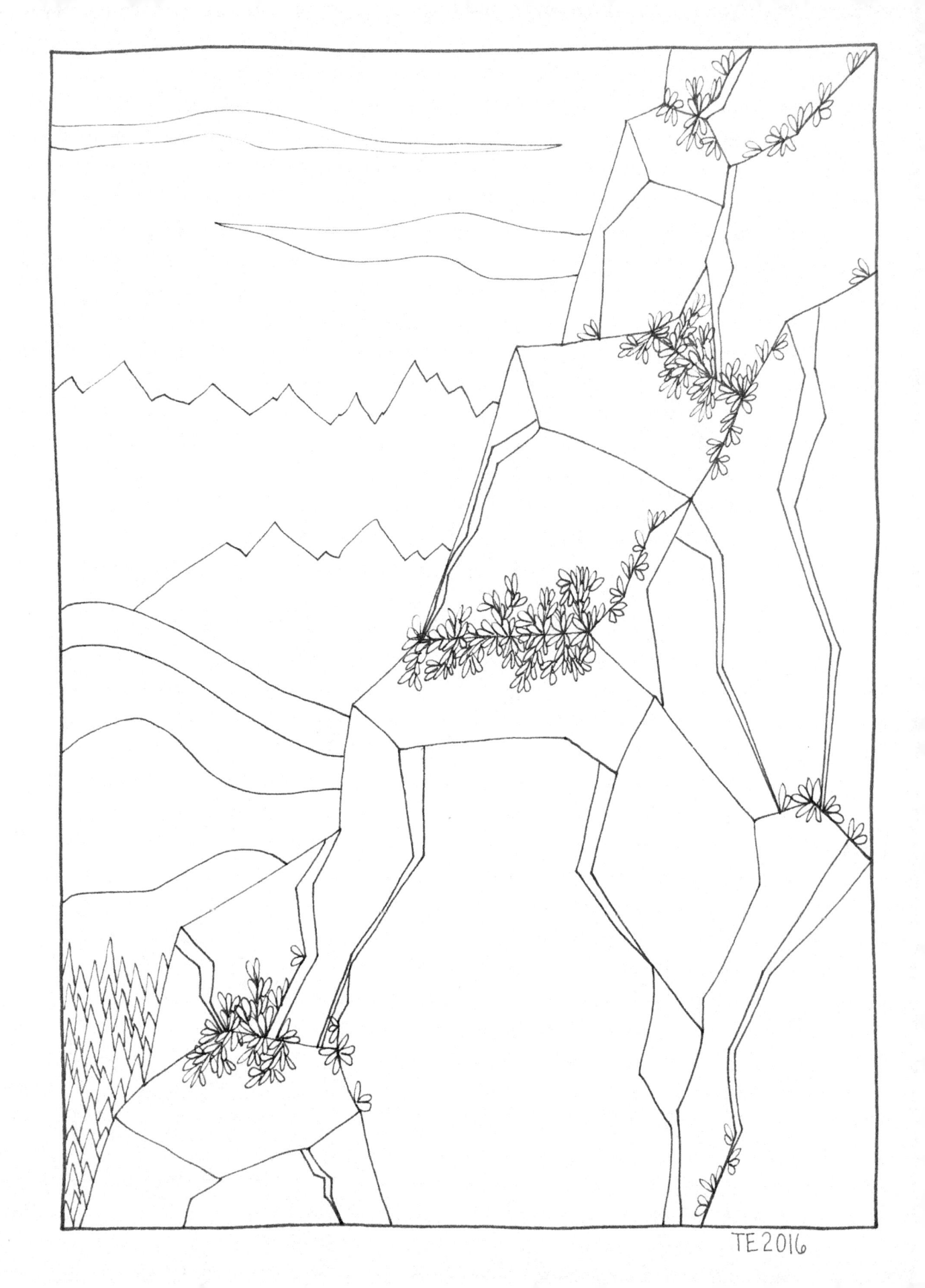

TE 2016

TE 2016

TE 2016

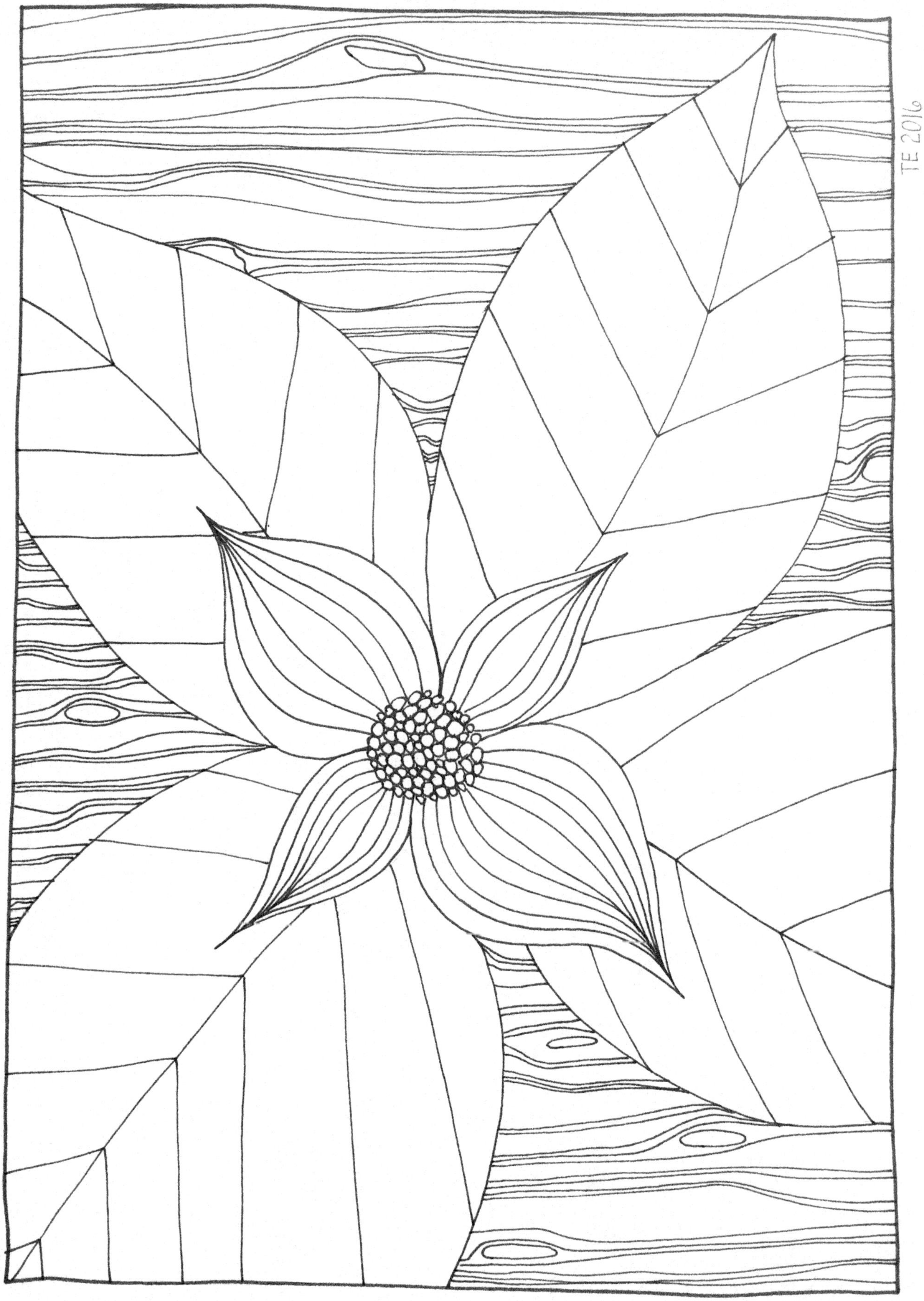
TE 2016

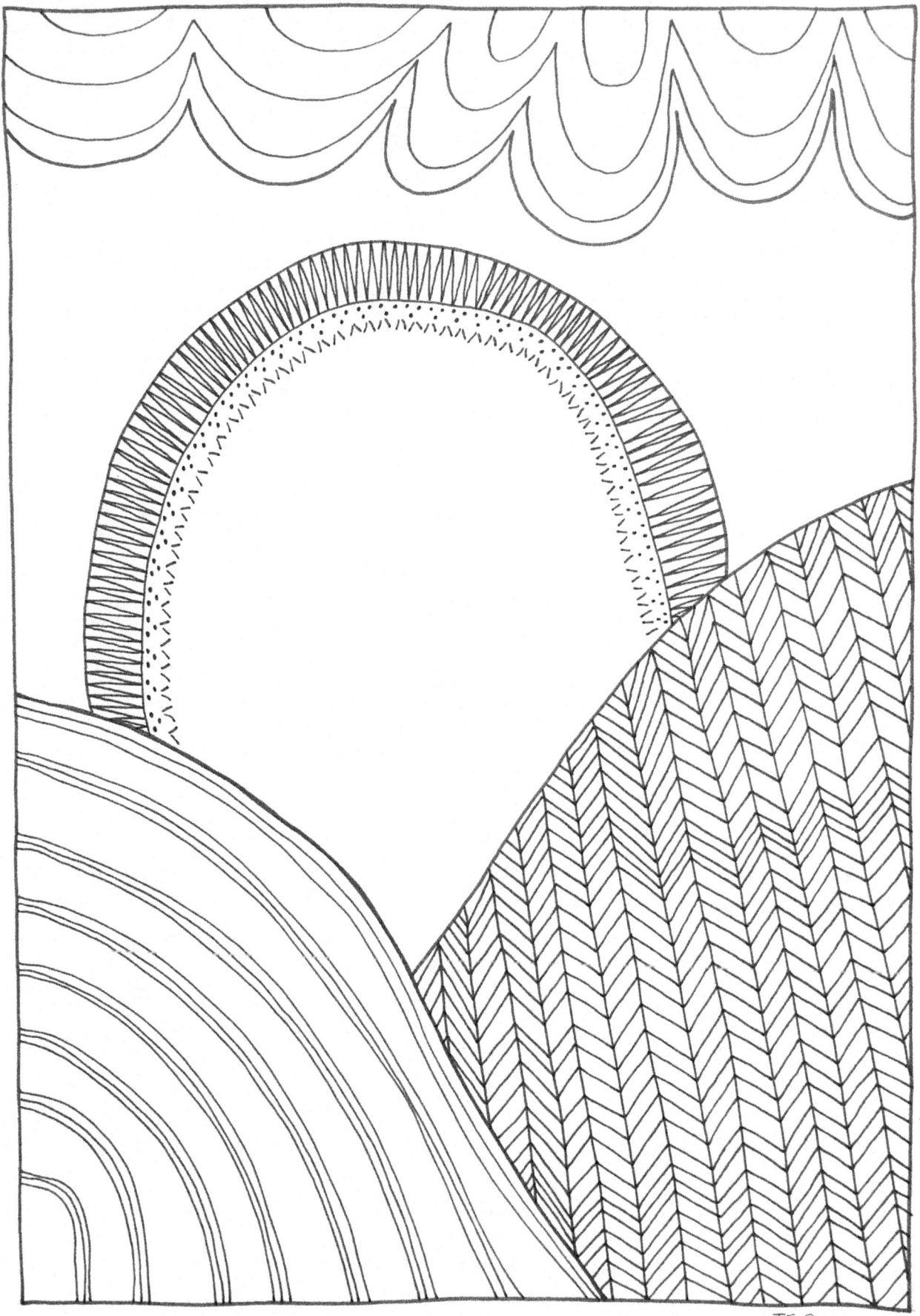

TE 2016

TE 2016

TE 2016

TE 2016

TE 2016

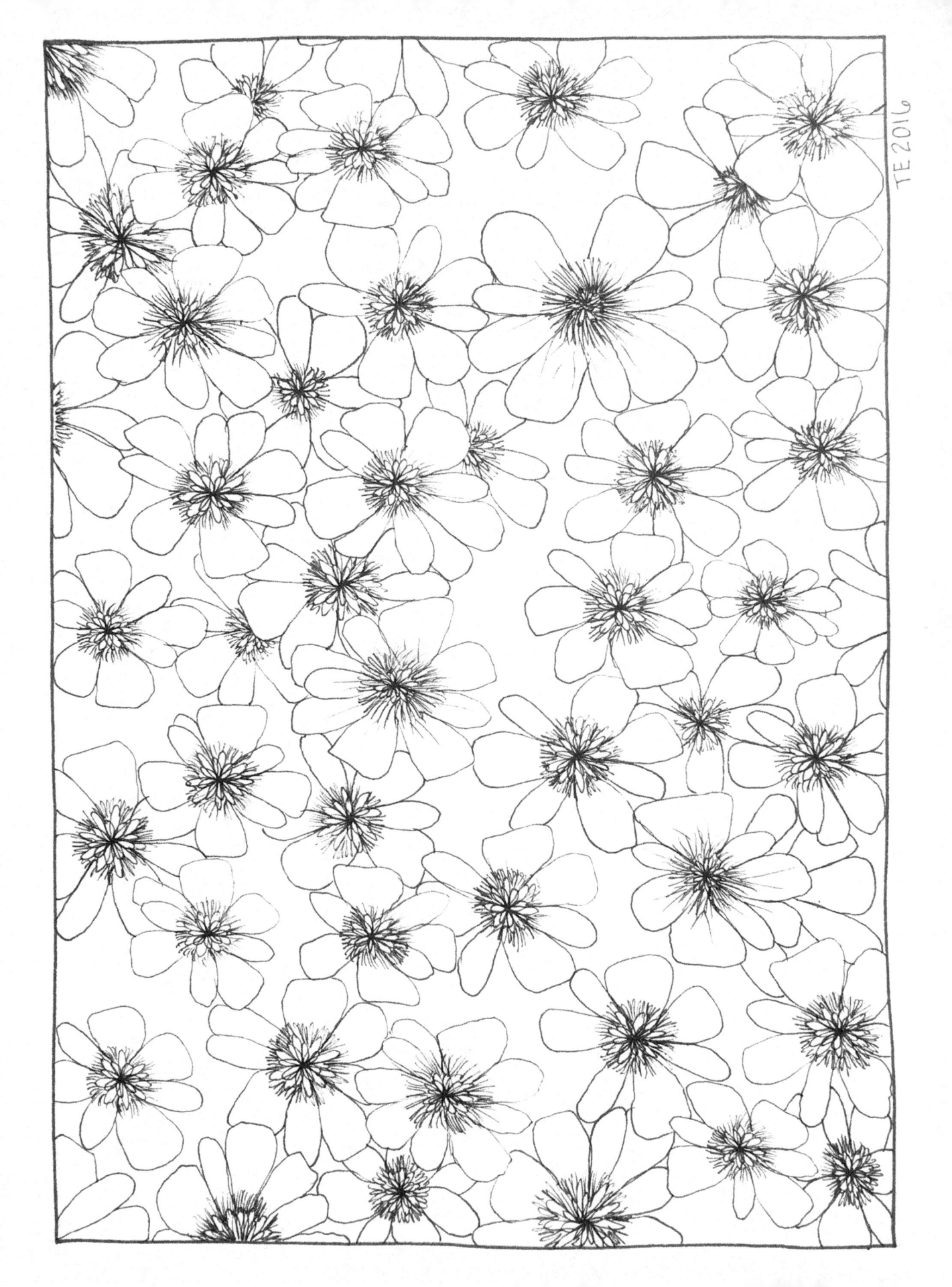

TE 2016

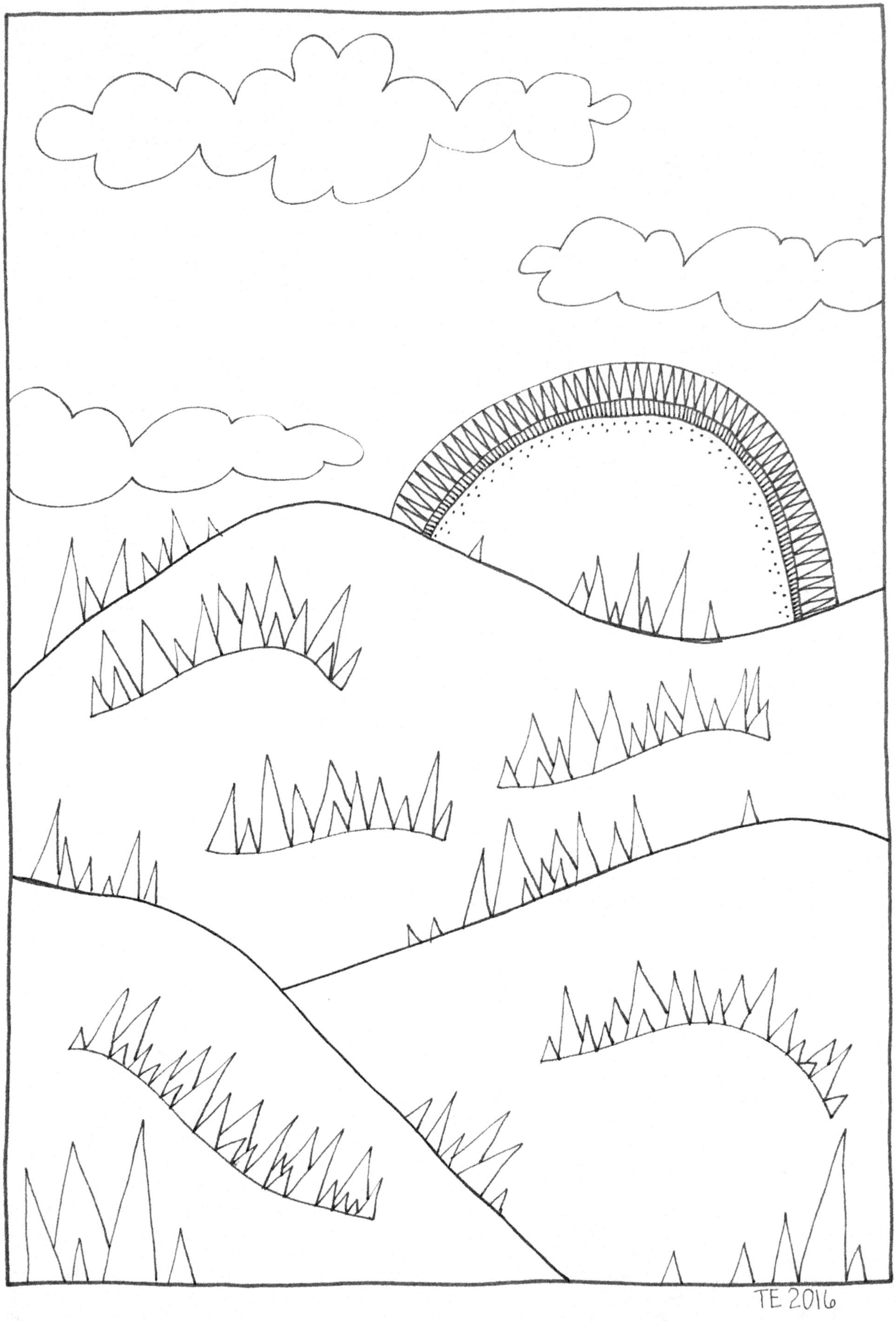
TE 2016

TE 2016

TE 2016

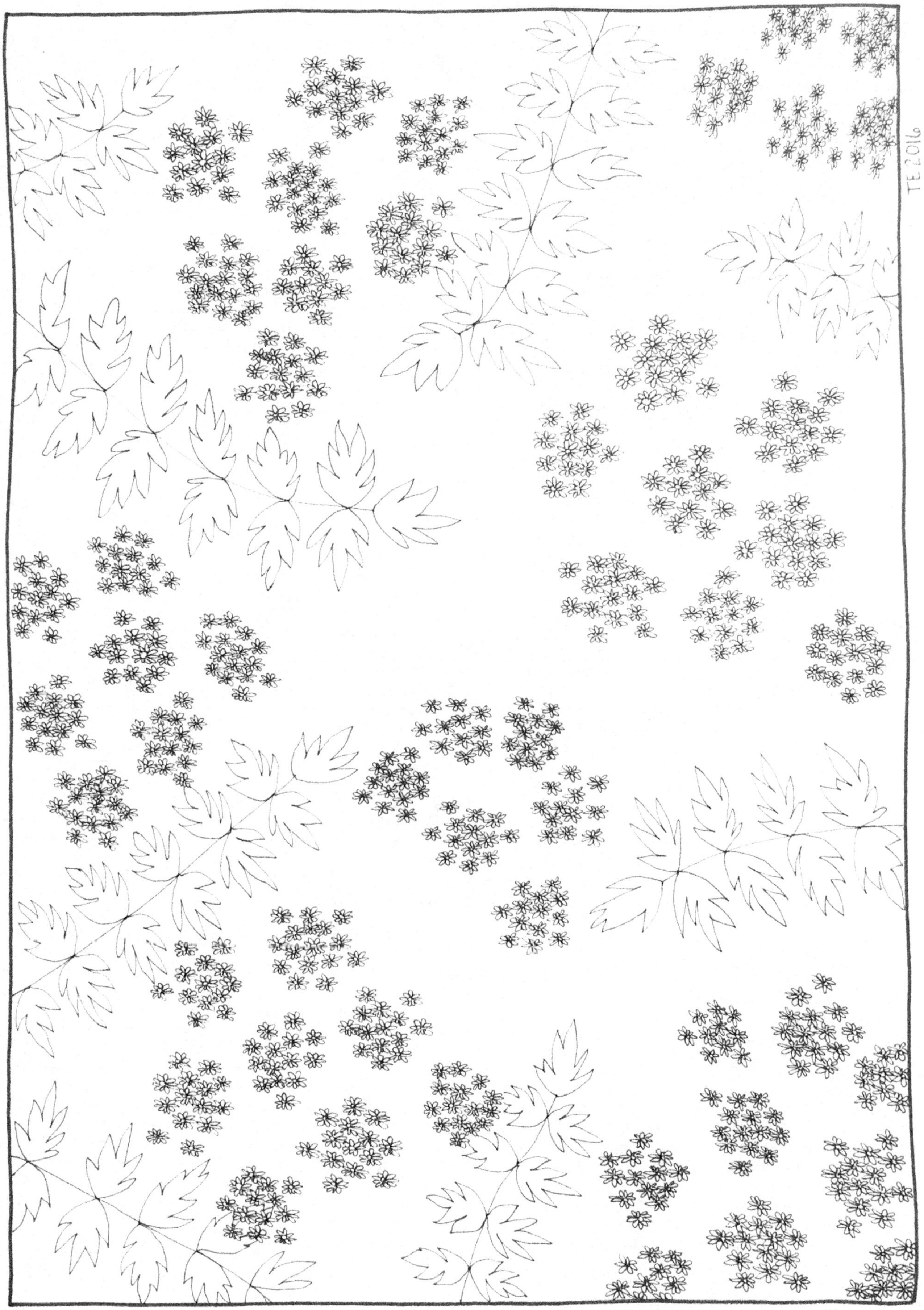
TE 2016

TE 2016

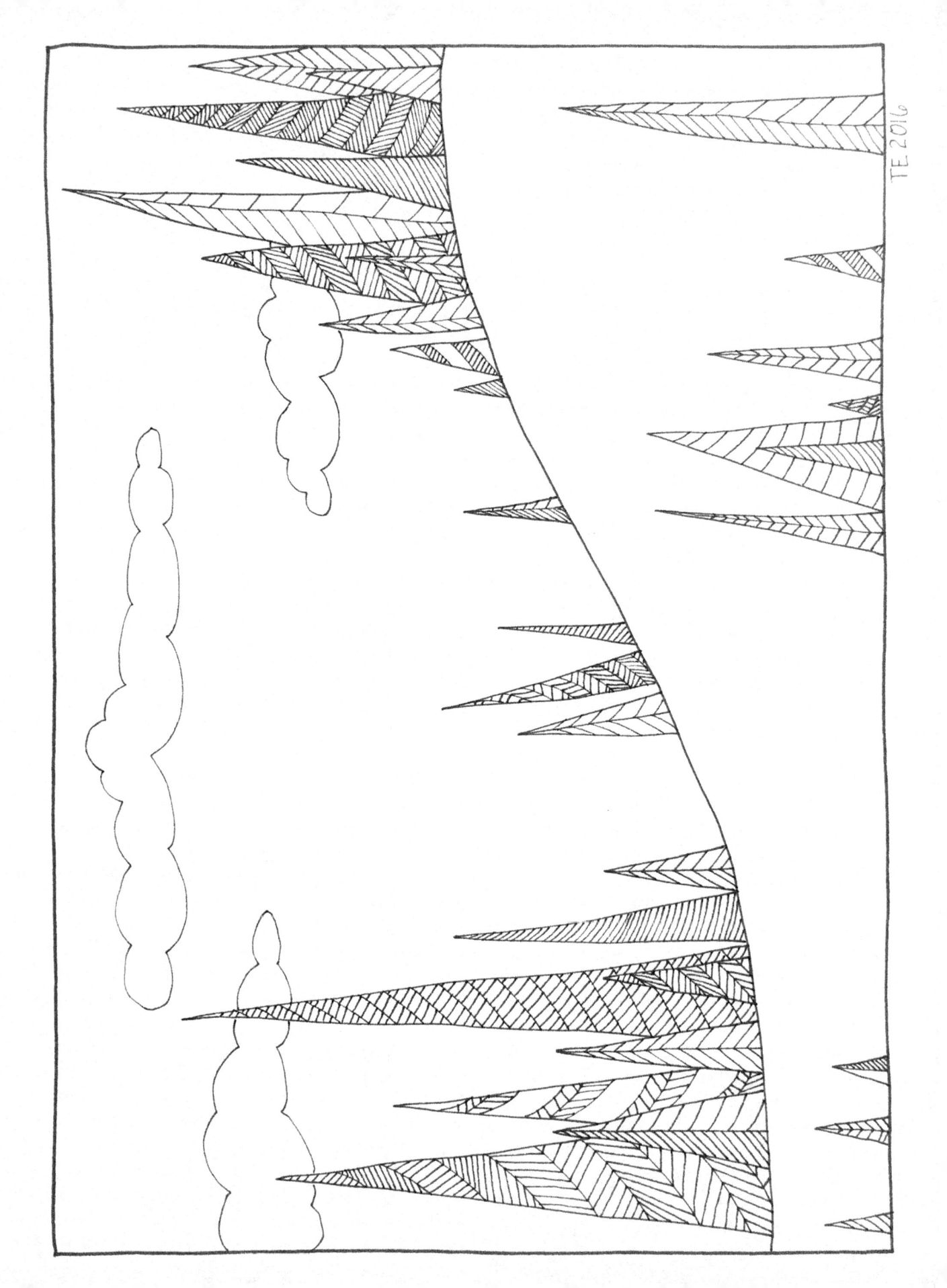

TE 2016

TE 2016

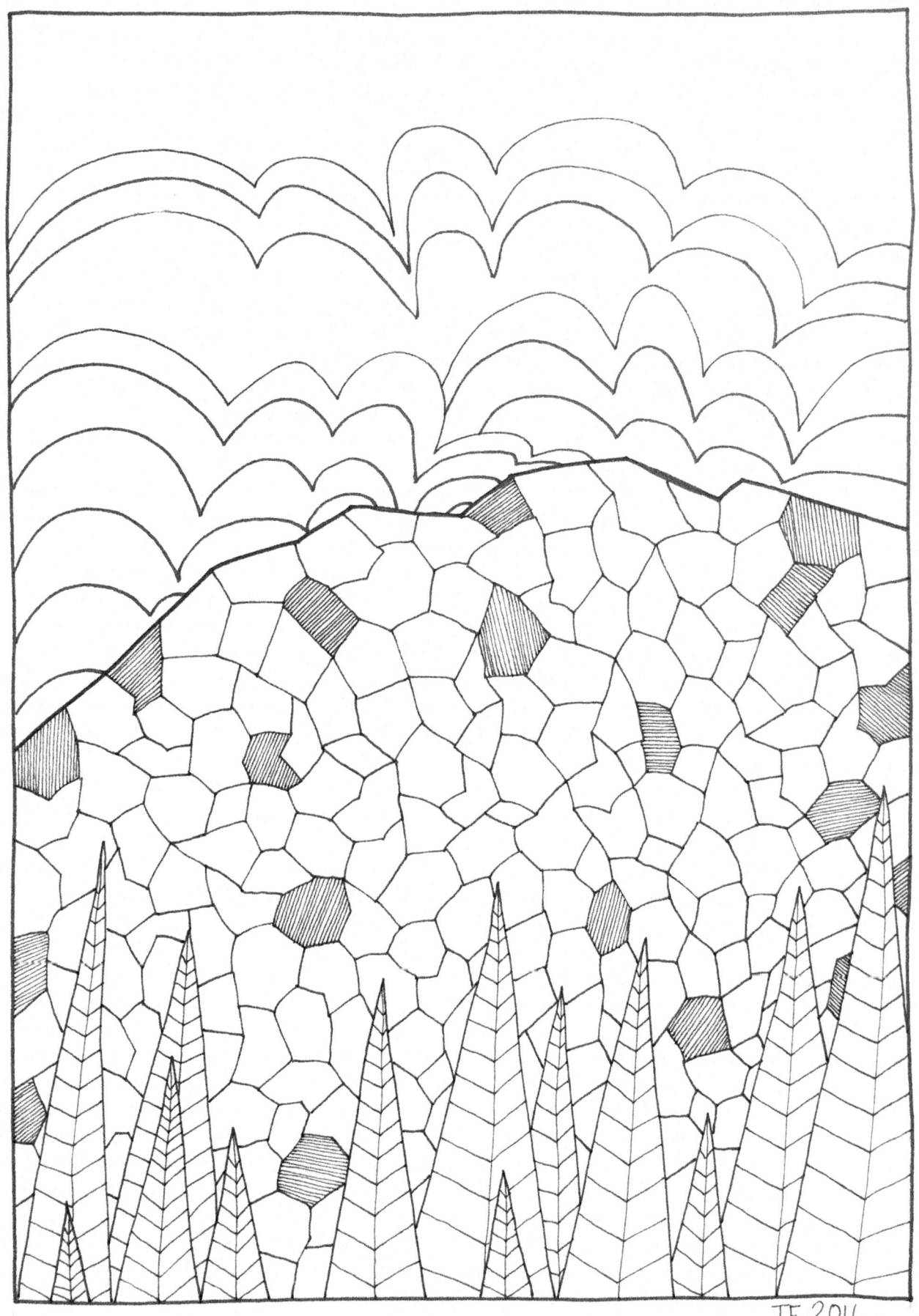

TE 2016

TE 2016

TE 2016

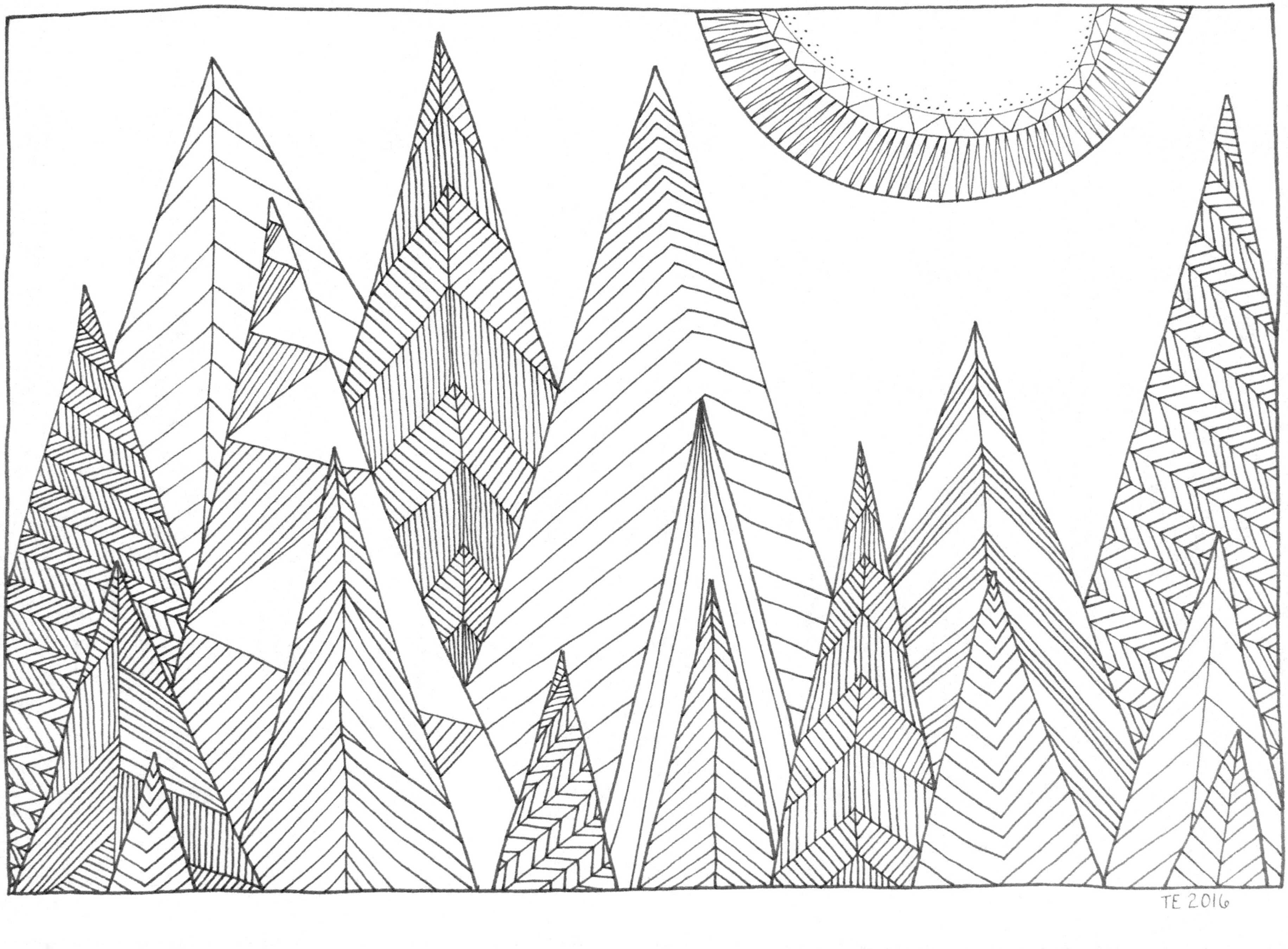
TE 2016

TE 2016

TE 2016

TE 2016

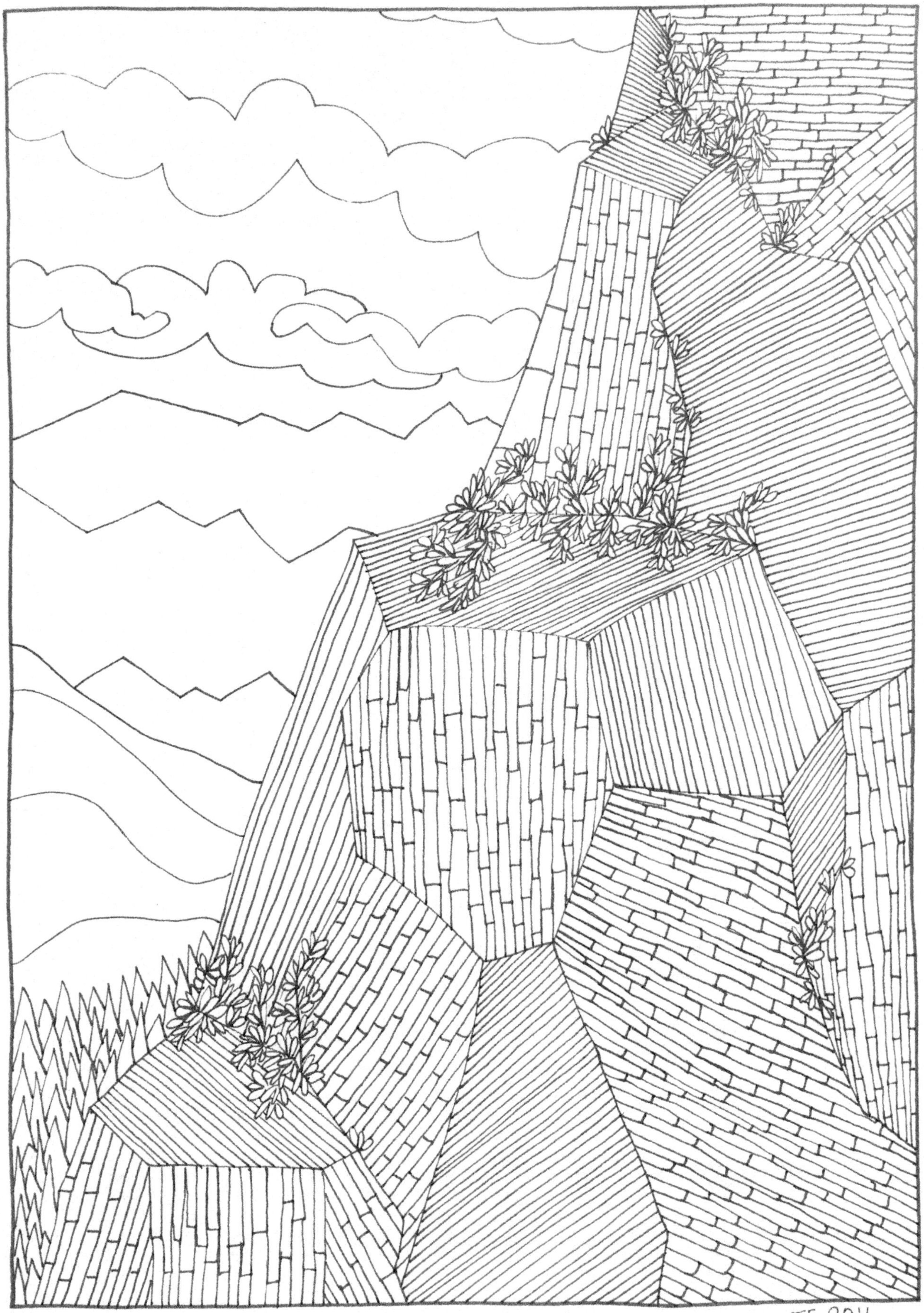

TE 2016

TE 2016

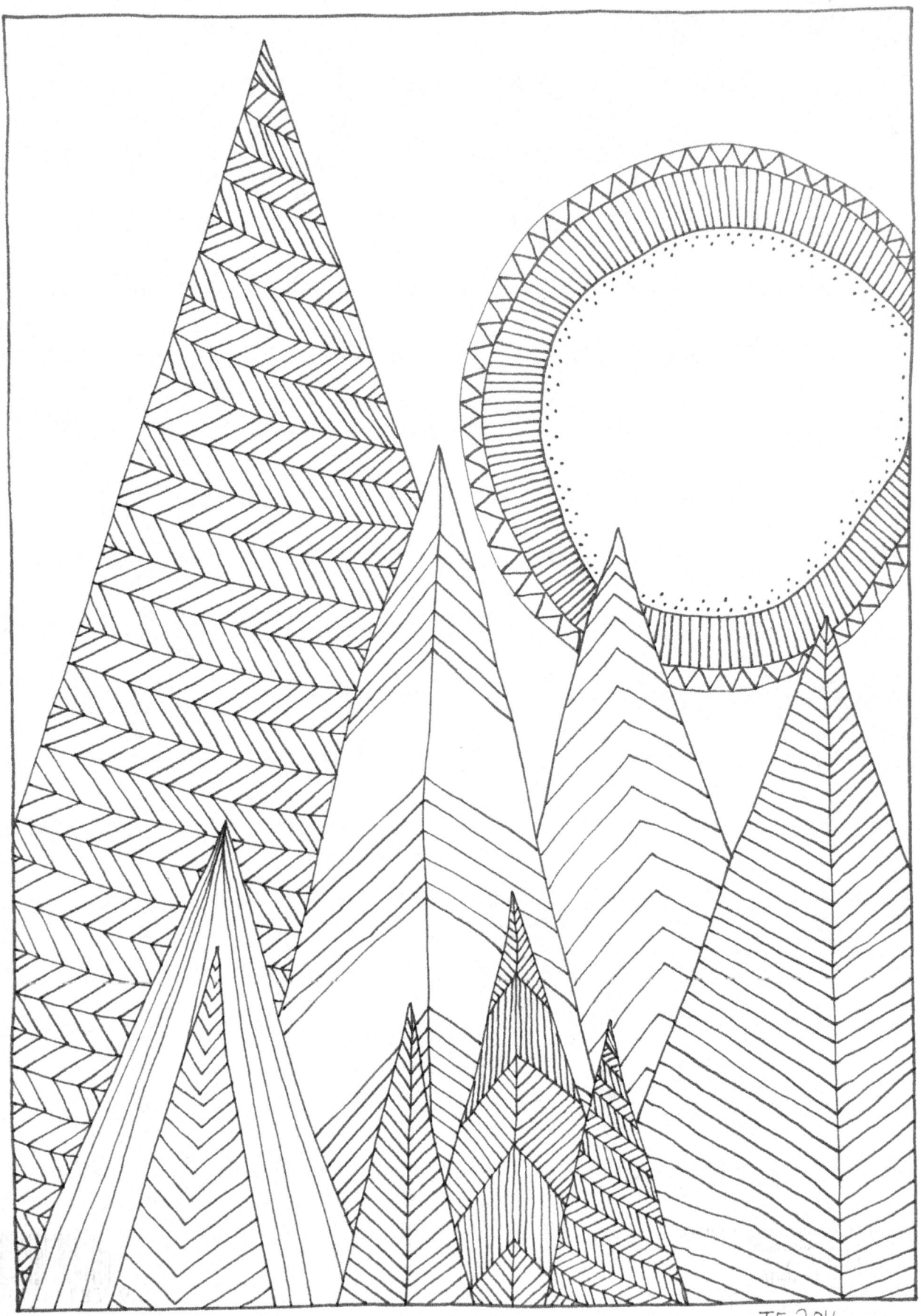

TE 2016

CPSIA information can be obtained
at www.ICGtesting.com
Printed in the USA
FSOW04n0915010416
18715FS